THE ABCs

OF STORYTELLING FOR YOUNG WRITERS

By Jessa R. Sexton, M.Ed. and Dr. K. Mark Hilliard

With illustrations by
Shelby Burr, Whitnee Clinard, and Jack Sexton

THE ABCS OF STORYTELLING FOR YOUNG WRITERS

Copyright 2019 The Hilliard Institute
ISBN 978-0-9990090-9-3

Written by Jessa R. Sexton and K. Mark Hilliard
Illustrated by Jack Sexton
With coloring pages by Shelby Burr
With infographics by Whitnee Clinard
Book Design by Whitnee Clinard
Edited by Rosemary J. Hilliard and Katherine Russell

All rights reserved. No part of this publication may be reproduced or transmitted in any form or by any means without written permission of the author.

Published by
Hilliard Press
a division of
The Hilliard Institute for Educational Wellness

Franklin, Tennessee
Oxford, England
www.hilliardinstitute.com

TABLE OF CONTENTS

A = author
B = bold
C = characters
D = dialogue
E = environment
F = first person vs third person
G = grammar
H = hero
I = inspiration
J = journal
K = keep writing!
L = lesson
M = mood
N = narrator
O = observe
P = plot
Q = quality vs quantity
R = read
S = setting
T = touch the senses
U = unique
V = voice and style
W = writer's block
X = delete (edit)
Y = you
Z = zigzag

Author

That's you! The author creates the story that is told. Sometimes writing is hard work, but if you love doing it—keep doing it.

Journal About This

Flip to the journal part in the back of this book to answer this question.

Why do you love writing? What are your favorite things to write about?

Bold Words

Being a writer means being bold. You have a story to tell, a poem to create, a song to compose. You know that words are powerful, and you're using that power to say something important or funny or beautiful—or maybe all three! Be bold. Write!

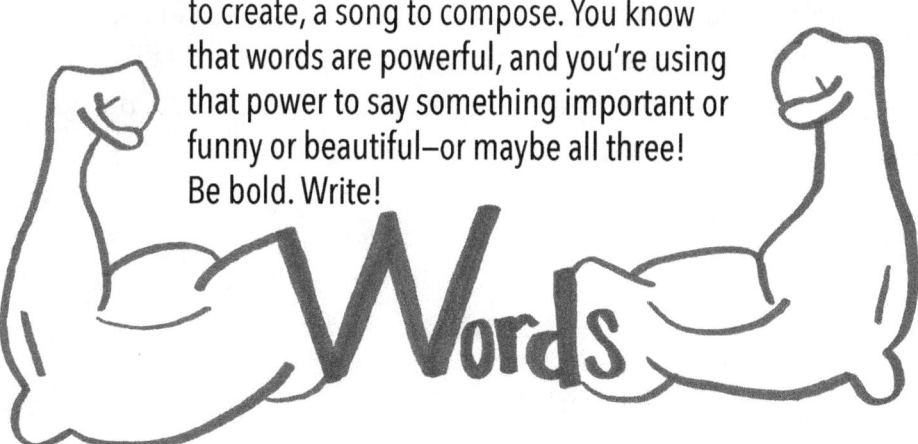

Characters

These are the people (or animals in some tales) in the story. Make notes for yourself about the characters—what they look like and their qualities. That way you will know them well so that you can *write* about them well. Remember: the characters are really the most important part of your story.

To make characters who feel like real people, use all the Elements of Characters shown in this drawing. That doesn't mean the first time you introduce each character you have to give all these details. And not every character you write about will be this well-defined. But you should share these things about your main characters.

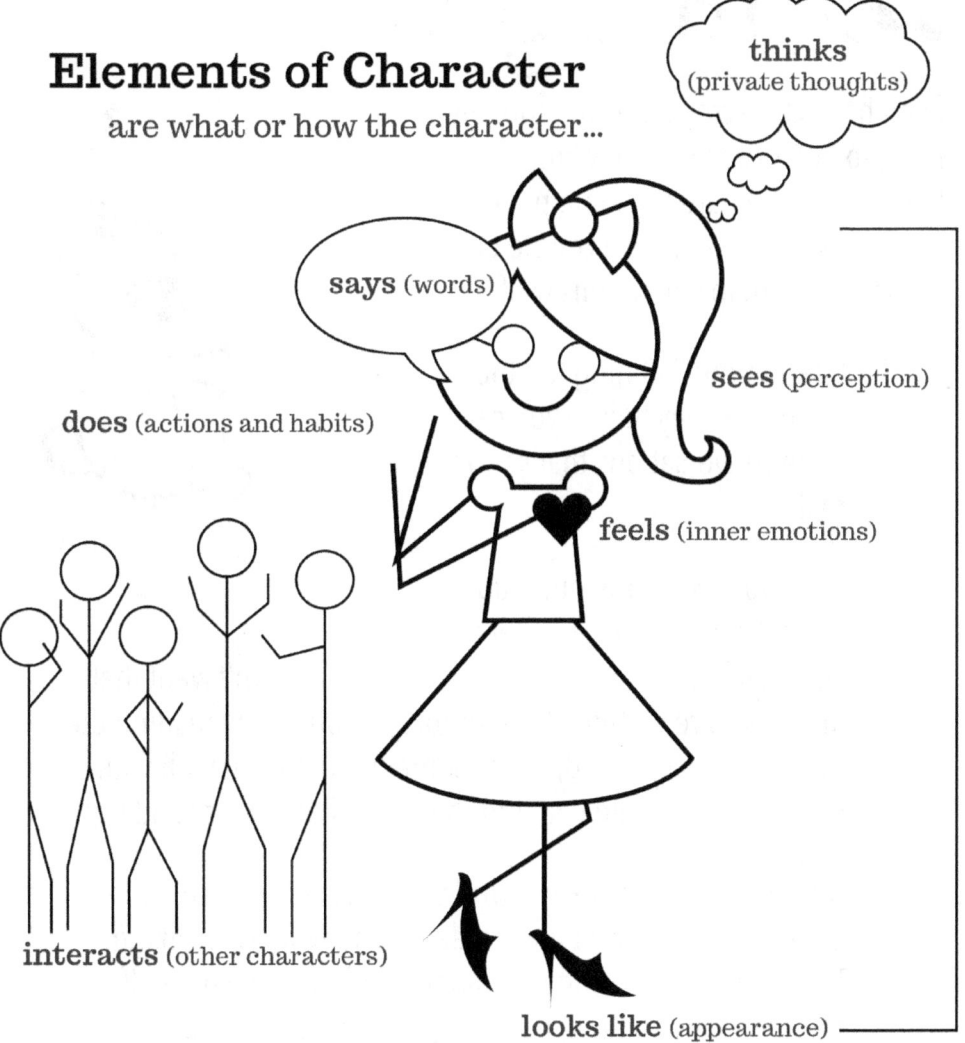

Dialogue

If you have characters, they're probably going to talk to each other. Writing dialogue can be hard for some people, but don't worry. There are a couple of tricks that can help you do this well.

1. Spend time listening to other people as they talk so you can write conversations that sound real.

2. Read your dialogue out loud. Does it sound stiff? In other words, like a bunch of robots chatting? You don't want that–unless you're writing about robots, of course. Try reading the conversation out loud, or ask someone to read it with you. Doing this can help you find the spots that don't sound right.

3. Be clear on who's talking. One of my favorite writers, who's super famous, wasn't always clear about who was talking. That's super confusing for readers. And that's no good. If I could go back in time, I'd tell him to fix that, pronto.

When you're writing, it may sound repetitive to keep saying things like *he said* and *she asked*, but it helps your reader follow the conversation. And, you don't have to use fancy words like *he exclaimed*, *she pondered out loud*, or *they whooped*. Most of the time, a simple said is the best. That way, readers focus on the dialogue and not on your fancy vocabulary.

Here's a little example showing you how to use spaces and clarity in dialogue.

"I'm writing a short story about zoo animals," Jack said.

"Are you koala-fied for that kind of writing?" June asked.

"June, sometimes your jokes are unbearable," said Jonas.

"Un*bear*able. Like a koala *bear*?" she asked.

Jonas rolled his eyes as Jack and June laughed.

Environment

The environment you write in is very important. We all have spaces where we can think and ponder and read and write our best. Maybe it's a quiet place outside–your tree house or a bench in the garden. Nature is often an inspiring spot to think and write.

Maybe it's in your bedroom, back porch, or just a special chair in your house. Maybe you like to have quiet music playing as you write, or perhaps you need it to be very quiet. Any of these environments is fine–it's just about what works for you. Try out different spots, then go with the one where you can write your best.

Journal About This

Flip to the journal part in the back of this book to answer this question.

Describe the perfect place you'd like to write.

First Person or Third Person

These words have to do with the point of view you're using to tell your story. First person means you're using words like "I" and "me" because the story is being told **by** a character, from his or her point of view. Third person uses words like "they" or "them" because the story is being told **about** the characters.

Grammar

Hey—sometimes grammar seems like a bunch of boring rules. But listen, you shouldn't worry about memorizing every grammar rule to be a good writer. And don't worry that the rules will keep you from having fun as you write.

Yes, you need to know the rules of writing, and you should learn grammar. When you know what punctuation marks mean, for example, you can use them to tell your story in the best way possible. It's okay if you don't have it all memorized. You'll learn more in school and can ask your teachers, parents, or other writers for help. Just remember, grammar doesn't hold you back—it helps move you forward into becoming a better writer.

Hero

Most stories have a hero. This doesn't mean someone in tights, a mask, and a cape. Not all heroes wear capes, you know. "Hero" is often another word for your **main or most important character**—the one who learns a lesson, beats a bad guy, overcomes an obstacle, and might even **appear** on the front cover.

Journal About This

Flip to the journal part in the back of this book to answer this question.

What are different things that inspire your writing or make you want to write?

Inspiration

Inspiration is everywhere! You just have to open your eyes and heart to see it. Figure out what inspires you to be more creative. Nature, quiet, music, books, art, conversation, tea time—give yourself time to enjoy the things that inspire you, and your creativity will soar.

Journal

A writer needs a journal. Keep it with you all the time. Maybe you'll write an entire poem, song, or story in your journal. Maybe you'll just make notes of words, phrases, character names, images, and other ideas that come to you. Even if it's just a few thoughts, write in your journal every day.

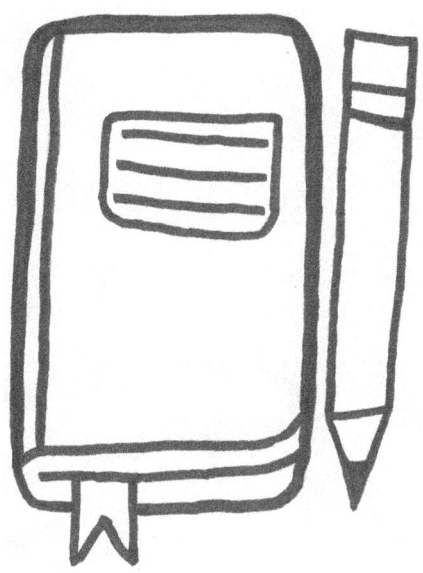

Keep Writing

If you want to be a writer, you need to write. That may sound crazy to say. I mean—of course you do! But even famous writers can have a hard time making themselves write in a steady routine. Writing is like music or sports—you've got to practice to get better.

But writing can give you a lot of emotions. Sometimes you'll feel frustrated because the words aren't coming easily. But if you love writing, try to remember that joy, even when you're frustrated or having writer's block. And just keep writing. Just keep writing.

Lesson

Some stories teach a lesson to the reader. Fairy tales do this a lot: they create a story with fantasy creatures or magic to teach a lesson. Think about "Little Red Riding Hood." Her mother tells her to stay on the path while going to Grandma's. Little Red disobeys and gets herself and her grandmother eaten by a wolf in the process! That's quite the punishment. Thank goodness for that lumberjack who saves them. Even still, one lesson of the story is to obey your parents.

Maybe you want to teach your readers about the power of imagination, friendships, the value of hard work, or believing in yourself. Or maybe you just want to tell a fun story with no lesson at all. That was the goal of math professor Lewis Carroll when he wrote *Alice's Adventures in Wonderland*. Though he didn't try to teach a lesson, he still wrote an incredible story more than 100 years ago that we still read today. Not bad, Mr. Carroll. Not bad at all.

Mood

There are places in every story where you need to help readers feel certain emotions. Your job as the writer is to set the mood for these emotions, making readers feel happy or sad or angry or afraid. You do this with your words: the nouns, verbs, adjectives, and adverbs you pick. Use emotional words that make people feel what you're talking about. Make your words come alive. Say them out loud or read them to someone else to see if you've helped set the right mood.

How do you find the right words to set the right mood? Look through a thesaurus. Here you can see multiple words that mean the same thing, but some will make you feel stronger emotions. Saying someone is *mad* means the same thing as saying someone is *livid*, but the last one has more emotion. Remember, it's not about using words no one knows or showing off; it's about setting the mood with your words.

A good writing exercise is to write in your journal when you're feeling a certain emotion, so later you can talk about it in your story.

Journal About This

Flip to the journal part in the back of this book to answer this question.

> Write down some emotions like happy, sad, angry, afraid. Then brainstorm words that go with them. For example: happy = smile, laughter, joy, sunshine ...

Narrator

So you're the one writing the story, the author. The person you create to *tell* that story is called the narrator. If you decide to make the narrator a character who's part of the story and using words like "I," "me," and "we," that's first person point-of-view, like we talked about in the letter F!

Observe

The best writers observe their surroundings. So start watching, listening, and making notes in your journals to help you remember what you observe. If you see or hear a new word, view a new activity, meet someone new, or go to a new place—always observe these things and write about them for use in your future stories.

Spend time just watching and listening. Write down details about what you see and hear, and also your thoughts and feelings. Did something make you feel happy, sad, hungry, strong, or weak? Try to explain those feelings with words.

Watch and write. Listen and write. And create opportunities for observing by planning and then going to new places and on new adventures.

Plot

The plot means *what happens in the story*. The plot starts with the introduction, or exposition. This sets the scene and gives readers any background information they need to move into your story. Some stories start right in the middle of the action, without a lot of introduction. That's fine, as long as you plan on giving the details at some point. Your reader needs to be able to understand your story.

A story needs a conflict, another part of the plot. Conflict doesn't mean an argument or a fight; it just means a character has a problem. The problem could be a situation or another person—sometimes the "bad guy." Often the story is about the character or characters trying to overcome or fix this problem. Usually other characters come in to help in some way, or to make the problem worse.

In the end, the conflict finishes in some way. Maybe the problem gets worse and defeats the hero, the hero solves the problem, or someone else comes in and does the solving.

Think back to "Little Red Riding Hood." Little Red meets a bad guy: the wolf. She has a conflict: should she disobey her mom and take the shortcut the wolf shares with her? Duh. She shouldn't. But she does, and the problem gets worse! The wolf eats her grandma and her, making it seem like our hero has lost. Thankfully, the lumberjack arrives to save the day. Little Red learns her lesson, and the bad guy is beaten. The end.

That's an example of the pieces of plot in action.

Quantity vs Quality

You need to make every sentence count, make every word great, when writing a story. This means you're more interested in quality (writing well) than quantity (writing a lot).

Always review your story. Re-read your story over and over and over. Ask yourself if you've used more words to explain something than you need to. Make sure others read your story also. Then make the changes needed to make your story even better.

Remember, it's better to have fewer words that are magnificent, than many words that are weak. It's better to have a wonderful short story, than a boring book. Don't worry about writing a lot—focus on writing well.

Read

Dr. Seuss once said "The more that you read, the more things you will know. The more that you learn, the more places you go." If you want to be a young writer, spend lots of time reading different types of stories.

The more you read, the better you'll write. You'll learn new words, how to put sentences together, what interests you the most, different styles of writing, and information about new topics. Be adventurous: try new styles and topics from what you usually read. Just like when you eat new foods, you won't like everything, but you don't know until you try. You might be surprised at what new thing you read and say, "Hey, this is great!"

Setting

The setting covers all the details of the place your story happens. You can set your story in a fantasy land: like the authors did when creating Narnia, the Secret Garden, the Hobbit's home in The Shire, or Peter Pan's Neverland. These are places we can only travel to through the pages and in our minds.

You can also set your story in an actual spot on the map, whether you name it the same or give it a fictional title. For example, you could write about your very own school and use those buildings as your inspiration, but call it something different.

When writing about your story's setting, think about the Elements of Setting illustrated on the next page. Some authors give details on all these elements; some give only a few. You have to decide how much your story needs. Just make sure you describe the setting enough to make it feel real for your characters and your readers.

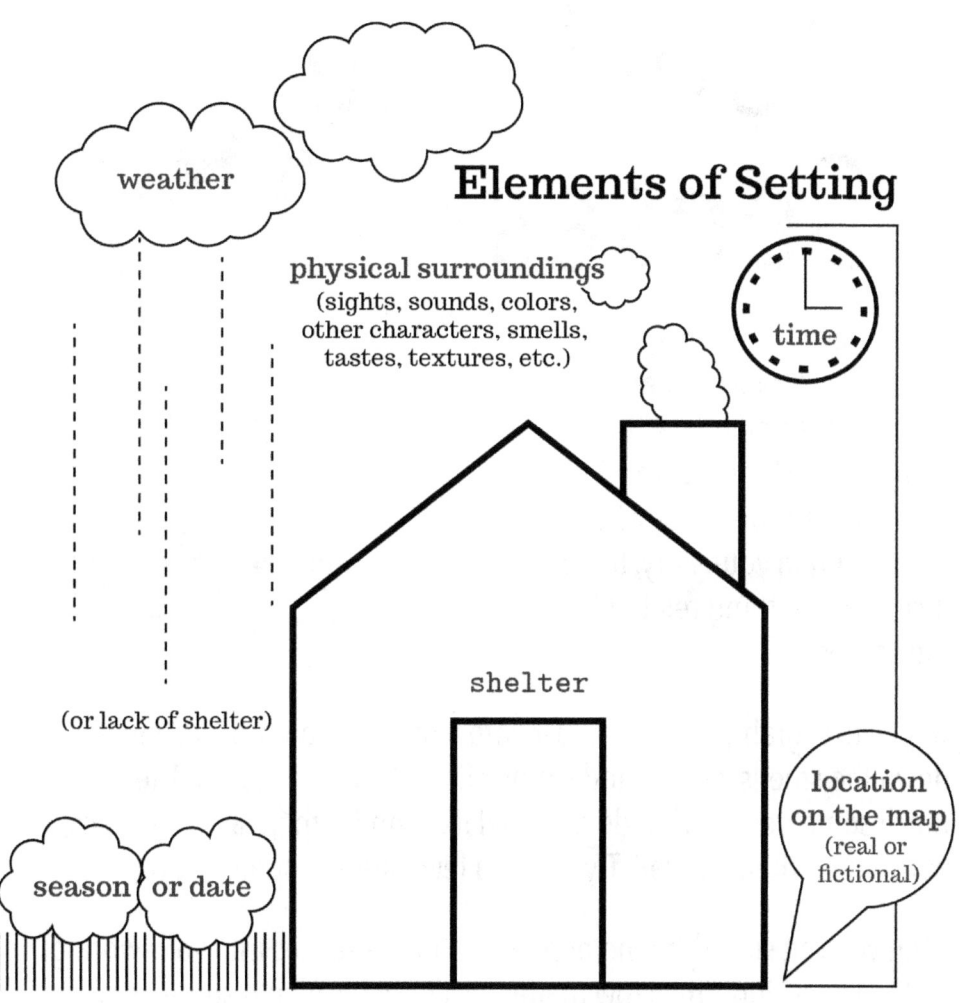

Touch the Senses

We all have five senses, and these senses are how we experience our world—smelling, tasting, hearing, touching, seeing. To help your reader experience what's happening in your story, try to include something related to all the senses.

To practice, grab your journal. Go into a room in your house, and write down the smells, sights, and sounds first. These are easiest. Then, touch some items. What do they feel like? And if there are any tastes, write about them as well. Try this in a few different spots.

Then you can start thinking of how to add the senses into your writing. Instead of saying, "the crow made noises," you can add some emotion and describe the specific sound: "It was as if the crow was talking to me personally, with his loud *Kraa, Kraa, Kraa*."

Describe how something is smooth, or rough, or ragged, or cold, or hot: "As I picked up the odd-shaped stone, it was so hot I had to toss it back down on the ground."

Make it clear how bright or dark a place is: "There was no light in the cave. I was in complete darkness. I couldn't even see my own hand as I waved it around in front of my face."

If someone can read your words about how the roses smell in a garden, and they can actually smell the roses in their head, you are becoming a good writer.

Unique

It's great to learn from writers. See how they do things, and think about what you like and don't like about how they tell stories, make poetry, or create a song. Then make your own unique creations based on the things *you* want to say, the characters *you* want to meet inside those pages, the melodies and lyrics in your own heart that you're ready to sing out loud.

This is what will make you unique. Because there isn't another you anywhere in this whole world–there never has been, and there never will be. If God gave you the gift of writing–use it in your unique way. You don't have to compare yourself to other writers–just work on making your writing better with lots of practice. Be the best version of you!

Voice & Style

The voice and style of writers is how their writing looks and sounds. Just like artists have their own way of painting or people have their own way of talking. Some writers are known for using lots of commas, and some use very few. Some writers focus their stories on action, and some on dialogue. These are parts of the way they write—their voice and style.

One of the best things about being a writer is creating your own voice and style. You use all the things we're talking about in this book to make *your* stories sound like *your* stories—not like anyone else's.

Writer's Block

Do you know what I have right now as I'm typing this? Writer's block. That's what writers call it when the words *just won't come*. This happens to everyone. Here are some helpful things you can do when it happens to you.

Just keep writing. That's what I'm doing now. I'm pushing through and writing anyway! I may have to go back and fix this part later, but I'm not giving up.

Write something different. Sometimes when I'm working on writing a book or a blog article, and the right words won't come to me, I try to write something different like a poem or a song. This keeps me writing, but gets my head out of the place where it's stuck.

Do something else that's creative. You can paint, dance, draw, sing, practice an instrument, color, or do something crafty. Doing one of these things keeps your brain in a creative place but gets you away from the writing that's tripping you up. That's why we've put in a couple of coloring pages for you in the back of book. Next time you feel writer's block, color one!

Do something else with your brain. Put together a puzzle, read a book, play a board or card game. Use your thoughts for something totally different.

Go out into nature. Take a walk, play sports, catch fireflies, or sit outside and just listen. Give yourself a break from your paper or computer.

Don't worry. Like I said, everyone gets writer's block. You will write again. See—I was in the middle of writer's block, kept writing, and I did it! I finished this whole letter W section. You'll get it back too. Just don't give up.

X = Delete

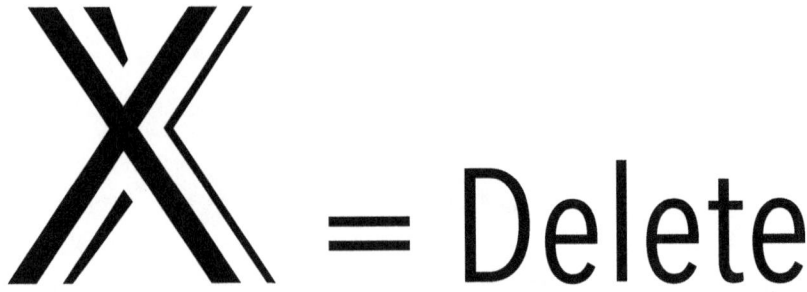

Don't be afraid to cut things when they don't work. This goes for ideas, characters, words, and even sentences. If you really love the part you're deleting, save it for another writing project!

I've said it before, and I'll say it again. Read your work out loud. This is how you'll find spots that don't sound right. Then you can fix them, or delete them.

All writers delete things from their work. All writers let editors read over and make suggestions. Do this too! Ask teachers, parents, or other writers you may know to look at your work and help you make it even *better*. Doing this makes *you* even better at writing!

You

We can all write better about the things we know, have experienced, and love. Your writing always has *you* in it.

Then, start experiencing new things so you have even more to write about. Real-life experiences are best (a school trip, a vacation, a visit to a zoo, a special adventure, a summer job, a sport, a game). But reading about experiences in books can help too. Ask your parents to take you on new adventures to learn more about things you want to write about. Visit new places together; try new things.

You are the energy behind what you write. The more you learn, experience, and feel, the better your writing will become.

Zigzag

When you're writing, you can do all the planning in the world. You can read this very book from cover to cover and decide you'll follow every piece of advice. You can journal every day and think you have your story figured out—and then you start writing, and things change. That's okay!

Writing can feel like zigzagging. You start in one direction, and then something sends you off in another direction. Maybe you don't have enough time to write as you thought, and the story takes longer to write. Maybe you start writing about four best friends and realize it would be easier to write well about just three.

If you're zigging along in your writing and hit a bump, don't be afraid to zag. Sometimes our best writing happens when we least expect or plan it. As we said before—just keep writing! If you come up on that bump or get busy in other areas of life, it's okay to slow down. But come back to your writing.

Being a writer doesn't always happen in a perfect, straight line. It's often a zigzag. But you're a writer. You know that even when writing isn't easy, it's still worth it. And you can proudly tell others you're an author: all the way from A to Z.

Journal About This

Flip to the journal part in the back of this book to answer this question.

Now that you're done with the book, what was the biggest thing you learned?

About the Woodfine Young Writers Guild

The Woodfine Young Writers Guild is a division of the Hilliard Institute for Educational Wellness and Hilliard Press. The purpose of the Guild is to advance literacy skills and encourage a love for reading and writing in young people.

While a well-recognized organization in England, guilds aren't that common in the United States. A guild is a group of artists or craftsmen who pass on their skills, talents, and knowledge by teaching their trade to the next generation.

This Guild is named after Dr. David Woodfine, a beloved educator in Oxford, England, and the Chancellor of the Hilliard Institute for Educational Wellness. He served in many roles within the University of Oxford system and taught in other educational systems in England and America. The author of five published books, two written for children, he has a background of training young people to learn to love the process of learning and to make their goals a reality in their chosen careers.

A Note from Dr. Woodfine

There is nothing more rewarding than creating your own story. Using your imagination can be lots of fun and can give pleasure to you and to others who read your creation. The thing is to be smart and make a start! No matter how long or short your story may be, put pen to paper. The results will be very rewarding.

So get started! Write!!

THERE ISN'T ANOTHER YOU IN THIS WHOLE WIDE WORLD

Attributions

Dr. Seuss. *I Can Read with My Eyes Shut!* New York: Harper Collins, 2018. Print.

Cover created with the usage of vector illustrations from www.vecteezy.com

Journal

www.ingramcontent.com/pod-product-compliance
Lightning Source LLC
Chambersburg PA
CBHW070040070426
42449CB00012BA/3114